Venus Bay

Julie Mitchell
Mal Chambers

Australia • Brazil • Japan • Korea • Mexico • Singapore • Spain • United Kingdom • United States

Venus Bay

Fast Forward
Purple Level 19

Text: Julie Mitchell
Illustrations: Mal Chambers
Editor: Johanna Rohan
Designer: Vonda Pestana
Series designer: James Lowe
Production controller: Seona Galbally
Audio recordings: Juliet Hill, Picture Start
Spoken by: Matthew King and Abbe Holmes
Reprint: Siew Han Ong

ISBN 978 0 17 012647 2
ISBN 978 0 17 012645 8 (set)

Cengage Learning Australia
Level 7, 80 Dorcas Street
South Melbourne, Victoria Australia 3205
Phone: 1300 790 853

Cengage Learning New Zealand
Unit 4B Rosedale Office Park
331 Rosedale Road, Albany, North Shore NZ 0632
Phone: 0508 635 766

For learning solutions, visit cengage.com.au

Printed in Australia by Ligare Pty Ltd
7 8 9 10 11 12 20 19 18 17 16

Evaluated in independent research by staff from the Department of Language, Literacy and Arts Education at the University of Melbourne.

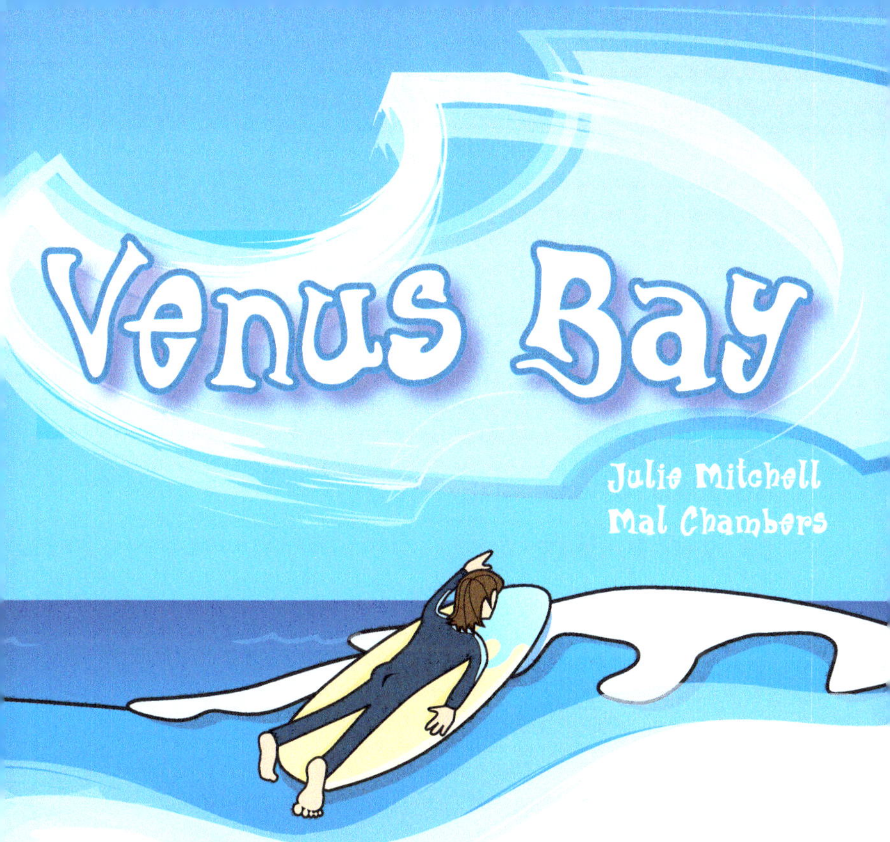

Contents

Chapter 1

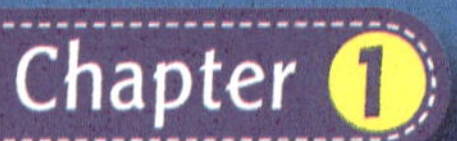

A SIMPLE FACT

Holly sat in the back seat of the car.
She was thinking about
her brother Jake,
as Dad drove the family
to Venus Bay.

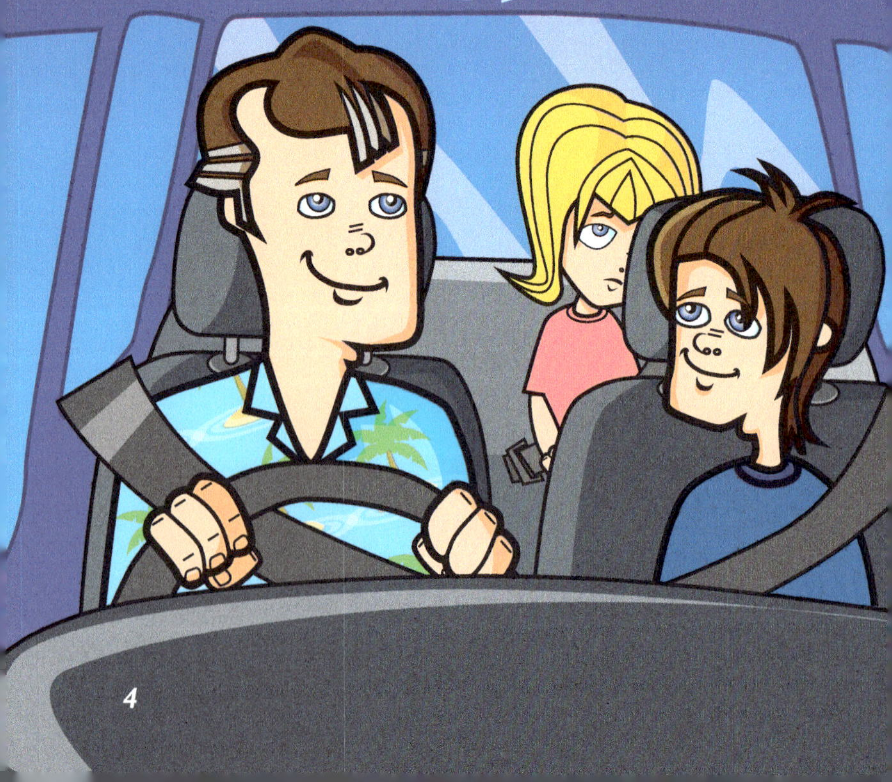

Jake used to be so easy
to get along with.
But lately, Holly had seen
a side of him she didn't like.

Jake had decided that Holly was weak.
When Holly tried to tell him
she wasn't weak,
he wouldn't listen.
"Don't get upset, Holly,"
Jake would say.
"It's a simple fact.
Just get used to it."

Well, Holly would show Jake he was wrong today.

Neither of them had surfed before, and Holly wanted to be the first one to ride a wave.

But, things didn't work out that way.

Soon after Jake entered the water, he was up on his board surfing, while Holly couldn't even stand up on hers.

"Give up, Holly!" Jake yelled as he paddled out to catch another wave.
"You're not strong enough to stand up and ride."

Holly frowned, and tried again. But, it was no good.

Running Words 168

Holly decided to rest for a moment.
She turned to watch her brother
come riding in on the next wave.

But, the wave passed
and Jake was nowhere to be seen.

Chapter 2

INTO THE SEA

Jake had fallen off his board
before the wave reached Holly.
But, that wasn't the worst thing…

In this part of the bay,
two powerful currents crossed
each other.
They made deep holes in the sand.
Jake was pulled into
one of these holes
when he fell off his board.

Down, down Jake was pulled,
as the sea roared around him.
Suddenly, it was dark and Jake realised
how deep the water was.

He struck out with his arms,
fighting the pull of the current.
Because it was dark,
he wasn't sure where
the surface was.

At last, Jake felt himself rising.
But there was another problem –
he wanted to take a breath.
No, he told himself,
and he tried not to think about it.

It was a long time before Jake saw light coming down through the water. He couldn't hold his breath any longer.

His mouth opened and the water rushed inside.

Chapter 3

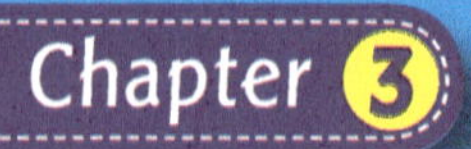

THE SEARCH

Holly knew something was wrong when Jake's board came tumbling past her.

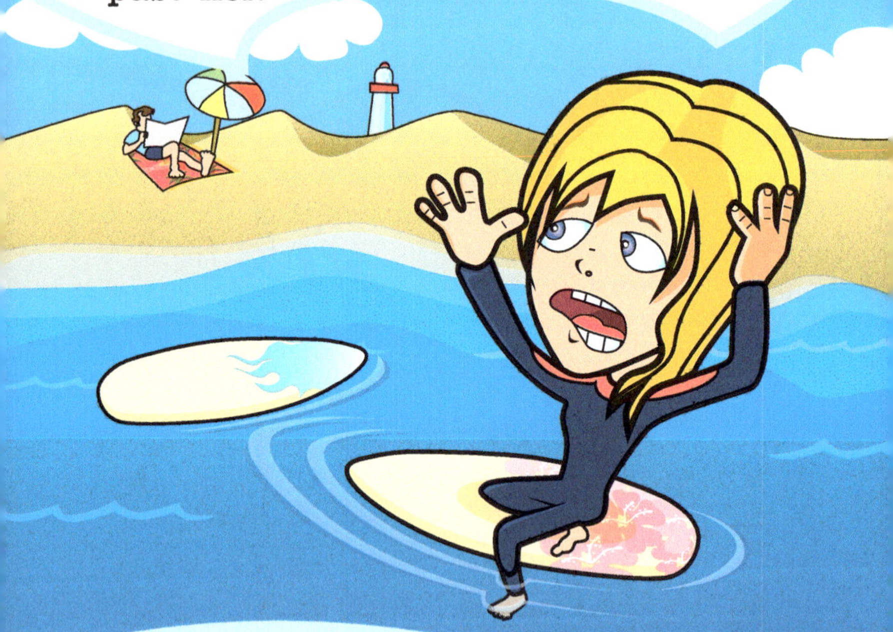

"Dad! Help!" she cried, waving towards the beach. Her father didn't hear her, or see her waving.

There was only one thing
Holly could do.
She took a deep breath
and dived beneath the surface,
searching for Jake.
She dived again and again,
but she couldn't see him anywhere.

Holly almost gave up.
But when she came up
after her third dive,
she spotted Jake floating face down
on the surface.

"Help!" she cried,
waving towards the beach again.
She swam over to her brother.

When she reached Jake,
she turned him face up.
Then, she began swimming
towards the shore,
carrying him against her hip.

It was hard work,
and Holly became tired.
Her arms and legs hurt,
but she refused to give up.

Suddenly, Holly's legs cramped, and she knew she couldn't carry Jake any further.

"No-o-o!" she cried.

Then, two strong arms took Jake from her.

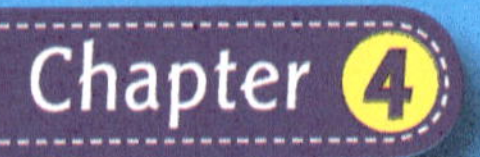

THE HOSPITAL

Dad had seen Holly waving.
He swam in to shore with Jake.
Holly rested for a while,
then she slowly swam in, too.

As she came out of the water,
Holly heard Jake cough.
"Is he all right?" she called
to her father.

"I think so," Dad said,
"but I'm calling for an ambulance."

Later, at the hospital, Holly sat close to Jake.

"You really scared me," she told him. "Thank goodness Dad came to help." She blinked back her tears. "I couldn't carry you any further. I just wasn't strong enough."

"Not strong enough?" Jake asked.
"You carried me most of the way in!"

Suddenly, his voice became soft.
"I'm sorry I ever said you were
weak, Holly.
If it wasn't for your strength,
I wouldn't be here at all."

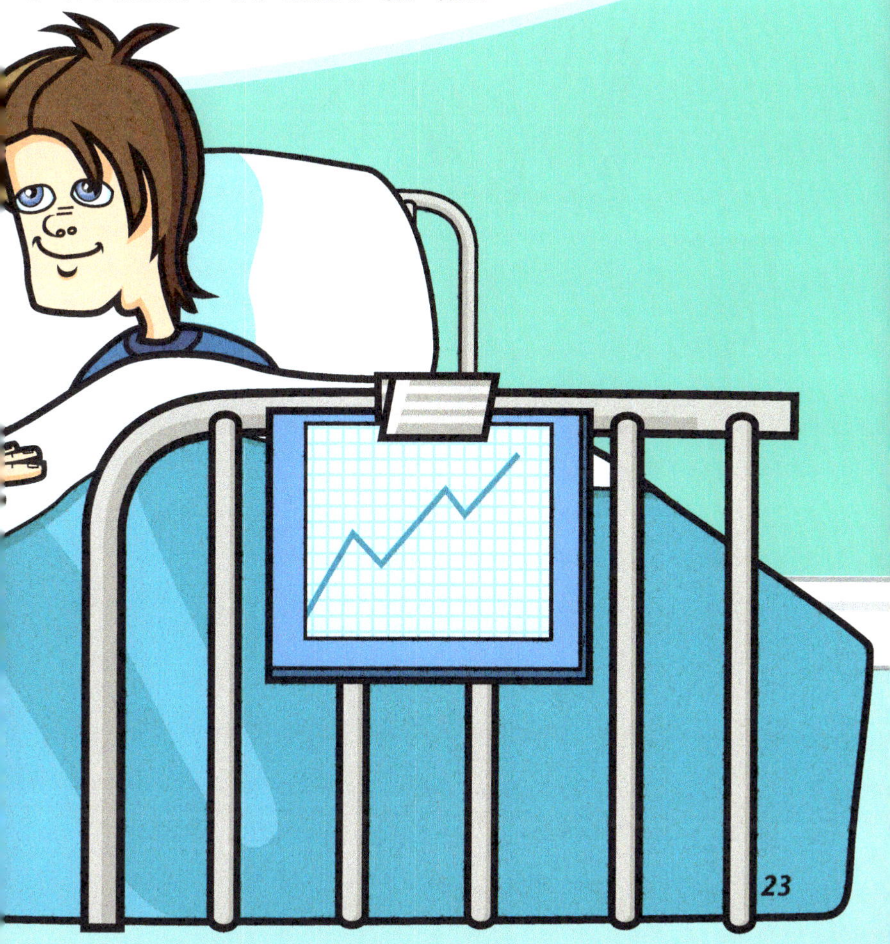

Holly put her arm around him.
"Well, Jake," she said,
"I'm glad you are."

And she meant it with all her heart.